Warming to Gold

Warming to Gold

DAVID H. ROSEN

RESOURCE *Publications* · Eugene, Oregon

WARMING TO GOLD

Resource Publications
An Imprint of Wipf and Stock Publishers
199 W. 8th Ave., Suite 3
Eugene, OR 97401

www.wipfandstock.com

PAPERBACK ISBN: 978-1-7252-5348-3
HARDCOVER ISBN: 978-1-7252-5349-0
EBOOK ISBN: 978-1-7252-5350-6

Manufactured in the U.S.A.   11/05/19

OTHER TITLES BY DAVID H. ROSEN

Henry's Tower

Time, Love and Licorice: A Healing Coloring Storybook

Samantha the Sleuth & Zack's Hard Lesson

Kindergarten Symphony: An ABC Book

The Healing Spirit of Haiku (With Joel Weishaus)

Clouds and More Clouds

Spelunking through Life: A Collection of Haiku

Living with Evergreens: A Collection of Haiku

In Search of the Hidden Pond: A Collection of Haiku

White Rose, Red Rose: A Collection of Haiku (With Johnny Baranski)

Torii Haiku: Profane to a Sacred Life

Look Closely: A Collection of Haiku

Medicine as a Human Experience (With David Reiser)

Transforming Depression: Healing the Soul through Creativity

The Tao of Jung: The Way of Integrity

The Tao of Elvis

Lost in the Long White Cloud: Finding My Way Home

Patient-Centered Medicine: A Human Experience (With Uyen Hoang)

The Alchemy of Cooking: Recipes with a Jungian Twist

Opal Whiteley's Beginning and Hoops & Hoopla

Drizzle—
star magnolia glistening

Eccentric elephant . . .
what a waterfall

Pouring rain
zap!
burst of light

Never again . . .
four years later,
will you marry me?

Living by the cleaners—
constant clouds

Pitch black . . .
where are my grandsons ?

My wife, Lanara,
a gardener forever . . .
flowers & veggies

Showy milkweed . . .
keep smiling

Post office . . .
long lines,
short chats

Disability . . .
waiting for
ability

Cold grey wind . . .
warming to gold

Slowing down
the pond's longer
circle

Spring oaks . . .
serenity
sparkling

Homemade pizza . . .
whatever's in the fridge
none better

God & Sophia hug . . .
birds everywhere

Went down under,
fell in love . . .
nature goddess

Distant sawyer . . .
in the garden :
artichokes & roses

Sauntering
hollyhocks and marigolds,
nodding

Leaf on tombstone
After death
more life

Faerie mound the wildflowers

My many seasons' friend . . .
the garden

Mr. Maynard . . .
threw me out of typing
enjoy the book

Leonard Cohen
makes it look
easy

Wind in the pines
angels whispering

Burning candles
hope is the Badlands

Spring snowfall
much loneliness

Out of warm house . . .
mandala moon

Young bamboo
no worries

Beyond the stones . . .
a waterfall

High on the hill
smile on it's face,
a cougar.

End to end sky
why despair
glimpse of heaven

My wife saved a bee . . .
more honey
David and Lanara Rosen

www.ingramcontent.com/pod-product-compliance
Lightning Source LLC
Chambersburg PA
CBHW072014060426
42446CB00043B/2543